50 BBQ Ribs & Grilling Favorites Recipes for Home

By: Kelly Johnson

Table of Contents

- Classic BBQ Baby Back Ribs
- Kansas City-Style Ribs
- Sweet and Spicy Grilled Ribs
- Memphis-Style Dry Rub Ribs
- Bourbon Glazed BBQ Ribs
- Honey Mustard Grilled Ribs
- Spicy Chipotle BBQ Ribs
- Smoked St. Louis Ribs
- Carolina Vinegar BBQ Ribs
- Jamaican Jerk Ribs
- Teriyaki Grilled Ribs
- Garlic Parmesan Grilled Ribs
- Lemon Herb BBQ Ribs
- Grilled Apple Cider Ribs
- Barbecue Spare Ribs with Peach Glaze
- Cherry BBQ Grilled Ribs
- Grilled BBQ Ribs with Mango Salsa
- Sweet Tea BBQ Ribs
- Grilled Baby Back Ribs with Pineapple Glaze
- Sticky Bourbon BBQ Ribs
- Grilled Ribs with Orange Glaze
- Korean BBQ Ribs
- Pineapple Teriyaki Ribs
- Maple Chipotle Grilled Ribs
- Cajun-Spiced BBQ Ribs
- Grilled BBQ Ribs with Whiskey Sauce
- Grilled Ribs with Brown Sugar and Mustard
- Texas-Style BBQ Ribs
- Grilled Ribs with Tangy BBQ Sauce
- Herb-Crusted BBQ Ribs
- Spicy Sriracha BBQ Ribs
- Smoked Bourbon BBQ Ribs
- Grilled BBQ Ribs with Spicy Rub
- Zesty Lime BBQ Ribs
- Grilled Baby Back Ribs with Cilantro Lime Butter

- Grilled Ribs with Sweet Honey Garlic Sauce
- Citrus Glazed BBQ Ribs
- Grilled Ribs with Spicy Peach Sauce
- Garlic and Rosemary BBQ Ribs
- Cajun Honey BBQ Ribs
- Sweet BBQ Grilled Ribs with Pecan Glaze
- Smoked Maple BBQ Ribs
- Grilled BBQ Ribs with Sweet and Sour Sauce
- Grilled Ribs with Chimichurri Sauce
- Slow Cooked BBQ Ribs
- Grilled Ribs with Smoky Tomato Sauce
- Grilled BBQ Ribs with Raspberry Chipotle Sauce
- Smoky Pineapple BBQ Ribs
- Thai BBQ Grilled Ribs
- Grilled BBQ Ribs with Roasted Garlic Sauce

Classic BBQ Baby Back Ribs

Ingredients:

- 2 racks baby back ribs
- 1 tbsp olive oil
- 2 tbsp brown sugar
- 1 tbsp paprika
- 1 tsp garlic powder
- 1 tsp onion powder
- 1 tsp chili powder
- ½ tsp black pepper
- 1 tsp salt
- 1 cup BBQ sauce

Instructions:

1. Preheat oven to 300°F.
2. Remove the silver skin from the ribs and rub with olive oil.
3. Mix brown sugar, paprika, garlic powder, onion powder, chili powder, pepper, and salt. Rub the spice mix over the ribs.
4. Wrap ribs in foil and bake for 2.5–3 hours.
5. Unwrap ribs, brush with BBQ sauce, and grill for 5–10 minutes until caramelized.
6. Serve warm.

Kansas City-Style Ribs

Ingredients:

- 2 racks baby back ribs
- 1 tbsp vegetable oil
- 2 tbsp brown sugar
- 1 tbsp paprika
- 1 tbsp chili powder
- 1 tsp garlic powder
- 1 tsp onion powder
- 1 tsp salt
- ½ tsp black pepper
- 1 cup Kansas City-style BBQ sauce

Instructions:

1. Preheat oven to 275°F.
2. Coat ribs with vegetable oil and rub with brown sugar, paprika, chili powder, garlic powder, onion powder, salt, and pepper.
3. Wrap ribs tightly in foil and bake for 2.5–3 hours.
4. Unwrap ribs, coat with BBQ sauce, and grill for 10–15 minutes, basting with extra sauce.
5. Serve with more sauce on the side.

Sweet and Spicy Grilled Ribs

Ingredients:

- 2 racks baby back ribs
- 1 tbsp olive oil
- 2 tbsp brown sugar
- 1 tbsp smoked paprika
- 1 tsp garlic powder
- 1 tsp cayenne pepper
- 1 tsp salt
- ½ tsp black pepper
- 1 cup sweet and spicy BBQ sauce

Instructions:

1. Preheat grill to medium heat.
2. Remove the silver skin from the ribs and rub with olive oil.
3. Mix brown sugar, paprika, garlic powder, cayenne, salt, and pepper. Rub spice mix onto ribs.
4. Grill ribs over indirect heat for 2 hours, flipping occasionally.
5. Brush with sweet and spicy BBQ sauce during the last 15 minutes.
6. Serve with extra sauce on the side.

Memphis-Style Dry Rub Ribs

Ingredients:

- 2 racks baby back ribs
- 1 tbsp olive oil
- 2 tbsp brown sugar
- 1 tbsp paprika
- 1 tbsp black pepper
- 1 tbsp salt
- 1 tbsp garlic powder
- 1 tsp onion powder
- 1 tsp cumin
- 1 tsp dry mustard

Instructions:

1. Preheat oven to 275°F.
2. Coat ribs with olive oil and rub with the dry rub mixture.
3. Bake ribs in a baking dish for 2.5–3 hours, covered with foil.
4. Uncover, and bake for an additional 15–20 minutes.
5. Slice and serve dry with your favorite sauce on the side.

Bourbon Glazed BBQ Ribs

Ingredients:

- 2 racks baby back ribs
- 1 tbsp olive oil
- 1 tbsp brown sugar
- 1 tbsp paprika
- 1 tsp garlic powder
- 1 tsp onion powder
- ½ tsp black pepper
- 1 tsp salt
- 1/3 cup bourbon
- ½ cup BBQ sauce

Instructions:

1. Preheat oven to 300°F.
2. Remove the silver skin from the ribs and rub with olive oil.
3. Mix brown sugar, paprika, garlic powder, onion powder, pepper, and salt. Rub onto ribs.
4. Wrap ribs in foil and bake for 2.5 hours.
5. In a saucepan, bring bourbon and BBQ sauce to a simmer until thickened.
6. Unwrap ribs, brush with the bourbon glaze, and grill for 5–10 minutes.
7. Serve with extra glaze.

Honey Mustard Grilled Ribs

Ingredients:

- 2 racks baby back ribs
- 1 tbsp olive oil
- 2 tbsp honey
- 2 tbsp Dijon mustard
- 1 tbsp brown sugar
- 1 tsp garlic powder
- 1 tsp smoked paprika
- Salt and pepper to taste

Instructions:

1. Preheat grill to medium heat.
2. Remove silver skin from ribs and rub with olive oil.
3. Mix honey, Dijon mustard, brown sugar, garlic powder, paprika, salt, and pepper to make the glaze.
4. Grill ribs for 2 hours over indirect heat, flipping occasionally.
5. Brush with honey mustard glaze and grill for an additional 10–15 minutes, basting with extra glaze.
6. Serve warm.

Spicy Chipotle BBQ Ribs

Ingredients:

- 2 racks baby back ribs
- 1 tbsp olive oil
- 1 tbsp chipotle chili powder
- 1 tbsp brown sugar
- 1 tsp garlic powder
- 1 tsp onion powder
- 1 tsp cumin
- 1 cup spicy chipotle BBQ sauce

Instructions:

1. Preheat oven to 275°F.
2. Coat ribs with olive oil and rub with chipotle chili powder, brown sugar, garlic powder, onion powder, cumin, salt, and pepper.
3. Wrap ribs in foil and bake for 2.5–3 hours.
4. Unwrap ribs, brush with chipotle BBQ sauce, and grill for 10–15 minutes.
5. Serve with extra sauce on the side.

Smoked St. Louis Ribs

Ingredients:

- 2 racks St. Louis-style ribs
- 1 tbsp olive oil
- 2 tbsp brown sugar
- 1 tbsp paprika
- 1 tsp garlic powder
- 1 tsp onion powder
- 1 tsp chili powder
- 2 cups apple juice

Instructions:

1. Preheat smoker to 225°F.
2. Rub ribs with olive oil and coat with brown sugar, paprika, garlic powder, onion powder, chili powder, salt, and pepper.
3. Smoke ribs for 4–5 hours, basting with apple juice every hour.
4. Unwrap ribs, apply sauce if desired, and grill for a few minutes for caramelization.
5. Serve with extra apple juice for basting.

Carolina Vinegar BBQ Ribs

Ingredients:

- 2 racks baby back ribs
- 1 tbsp olive oil
- 1 tbsp brown sugar
- 1 tsp smoked paprika
- 1 tsp garlic powder
- 1 tsp onion powder
- ½ tsp black pepper
- 2 cups apple cider vinegar
- 1 tbsp hot sauce

Instructions:

1. Preheat oven to 275°F.
2. Rub ribs with olive oil and a dry rub of brown sugar, paprika, garlic powder, onion powder, pepper, and salt.
3. Wrap ribs in foil and bake for 2.5–3 hours.
4. Mix apple cider vinegar and hot sauce. Brush ribs with the vinegar sauce after unwrapping them.
5. Grill ribs for 5–10 minutes and serve with extra vinegar sauce.

Jamaican Jerk Ribs

Ingredients:

- 2 racks baby back ribs
- 1 tbsp olive oil
- 2 tbsp brown sugar
- 1 tbsp allspice
- 1 tsp thyme
- 1 tsp cinnamon
- 1 tsp garlic powder
- 1 tsp onion powder
- 1 tsp cayenne pepper
- 2 tbsp soy sauce
- 1 tbsp lime juice
- 1 tbsp dark rum

Instructions:

1. Preheat oven to 300°F.
2. Coat ribs with olive oil and rub with brown sugar, allspice, thyme, cinnamon, garlic powder, onion powder, cayenne, and salt.
3. Mix soy sauce, lime juice, and rum and brush over ribs.
4. Wrap ribs in foil and bake for 2.5 hours.
5. Grill for 10–15 minutes and serve.

Teriyaki Grilled Ribs

Ingredients:

- 2 racks baby back ribs
- 1 tbsp olive oil
- 1 cup teriyaki sauce
- 2 tbsp brown sugar
- 1 tbsp garlic, minced
- 1 tsp grated ginger

Instructions:

1. Preheat grill to medium heat.
2. Rub ribs with olive oil and cook over indirect heat for 2 hours, turning occasionally.
3. Mix teriyaki sauce, brown sugar, garlic, and ginger.
4. Brush sauce onto ribs during the last 15–20 minutes of grilling.
5. Serve with extra sauce on the side.

Garlic Parmesan Grilled Ribs

Ingredients:

- 2 racks baby back ribs
- 1 tbsp olive oil
- 1 cup grated Parmesan cheese
- 4 cloves garlic, minced
- 1 tbsp parsley, chopped
- 1 tsp lemon zest

Instructions:

1. Preheat grill to medium heat.
2. Rub ribs with olive oil and grill for 2 hours, flipping occasionally.
3. In a bowl, mix Parmesan, garlic, parsley, and lemon zest.
4. Brush garlic Parmesan mixture over ribs during the last 10 minutes of grilling.
5. Serve with extra Parmesan.

Lemon Herb BBQ Ribs

Ingredients:

- 2 racks baby back ribs
- 1 tbsp olive oil
- 1 tbsp lemon juice
- 1 tbsp lemon zest
- 1 tbsp fresh thyme, chopped
- 1 tbsp fresh rosemary, chopped
- 1 tsp garlic powder
- 1 tsp salt

Instructions:

1. Preheat grill to medium heat.
2. Rub ribs with olive oil, lemon juice, lemon zest, thyme, rosemary, garlic powder, and salt.
3. Grill ribs over indirect heat for 2 hours, turning occasionally.
4. Serve with extra lemon wedges and fresh herbs.

Grilled Apple Cider Ribs

Ingredients:

- 2 racks baby back ribs
- 1 tbsp olive oil
- 1 cup apple cider
- 2 tbsp brown sugar
- 1 tbsp Dijon mustard
- 1 tsp cinnamon
- 1 tsp smoked paprika

Instructions:

1. Preheat grill to medium heat.
2. Rub ribs with olive oil and grill over indirect heat for 2 hours.
3. In a saucepan, combine apple cider, brown sugar, mustard, cinnamon, and paprika.
4. Brush ribs with apple cider glaze during the last 15 minutes of grilling.
5. Serve with extra apple cider sauce on the side.

Barbecue Spare Ribs with Peach Glaze

Ingredients:

- 2 racks spare ribs
- 1 tbsp olive oil
- 1 cup peach preserves
- 2 tbsp apple cider vinegar
- 1 tbsp Dijon mustard
- 1 tbsp brown sugar
- Salt and pepper to taste

Instructions:

1. Preheat oven to 275°F.
2. Rub ribs with olive oil, salt, and pepper, and wrap them in foil.
3. Bake for 2.5–3 hours.
4. Mix peach preserves, vinegar, mustard, and brown sugar for the glaze.
5. Brush peach glaze over ribs and grill for 5–10 minutes.
6. Serve with more peach glaze.

Cherry BBQ Grilled Ribs

Ingredients:

- 2 racks baby back ribs
- 1 tbsp olive oil
- 1 cup cherry preserves
- 2 tbsp apple cider vinegar
- 1 tbsp soy sauce
- 1 tsp ginger, grated

Instructions:

1. Preheat grill to medium heat.
2. Rub ribs with olive oil and grill for 2 hours over indirect heat.
3. In a saucepan, combine cherry preserves, vinegar, soy sauce, and ginger.
4. Brush cherry BBQ sauce over ribs during the last 15 minutes of grilling.
5. Serve with extra sauce on the side.

Grilled BBQ Ribs with Mango Salsa

Ingredients:

- 2 racks baby back ribs
- 1 tbsp olive oil
- 1 cup BBQ sauce
- 1 ripe mango, peeled and diced
- 1 red onion, diced
- 1 tbsp cilantro, chopped
- 1 tbsp lime juice

Instructions:

1. Preheat grill to medium heat.
2. Rub ribs with olive oil and grill for 2 hours, turning occasionally.
3. Mix mango, red onion, cilantro, and lime juice to make the salsa.
4. Brush ribs with BBQ sauce during the last 15–20 minutes of grilling.
5. Serve ribs topped with mango salsa.

Sweet Tea BBQ Ribs

Ingredients:

- 2 racks baby back ribs
- 1 tbsp olive oil
- 2 cups sweet tea
- 1 cup BBQ sauce
- 2 tbsp brown sugar
- 1 tbsp lemon juice

Instructions:

1. Preheat grill to medium heat.
2. Rub ribs with olive oil and grill for 2 hours.
3. In a saucepan, combine sweet tea, BBQ sauce, brown sugar, and lemon juice.
4. Brush sweet tea BBQ sauce over ribs during the last 15 minutes of grilling.
5. Serve with extra sauce on the side.

Grilled Baby Back Ribs with Pineapple Glaze

Ingredients:

- 2 racks baby back ribs
- 1 tbsp olive oil
- 1 cup pineapple juice
- 2 tbsp brown sugar
- 1 tbsp soy sauce
- 1 tbsp lime juice
- 1 tsp ginger, grated

Instructions:

1. Preheat grill to medium heat.
2. Rub ribs with olive oil and grill over indirect heat for 2 hours.
3. In a saucepan, combine pineapple juice, brown sugar, soy sauce, lime juice, and ginger.
4. Brush pineapple glaze over ribs during the last 10–15 minutes of grilling.
5. Serve with extra glaze.

Sticky Bourbon BBQ Ribs

Ingredients:

- 2 racks baby back ribs
- 1 tbsp olive oil
- ¼ cup bourbon
- 1 cup BBQ sauce
- 2 tbsp honey
- 2 tbsp brown sugar
- 1 tbsp Worcestershire sauce

Instructions:

1. Preheat grill to medium heat.
2. Rub ribs with olive oil and grill for 2 hours.
3. In a saucepan, combine bourbon, BBQ sauce, honey, brown sugar, and Worcestershire sauce.
4. Brush bourbon BBQ sauce over ribs during the last 15 minutes of grilling.
5. Serve with extra sauce on the side.

Grilled Ribs with Orange Glaze

Ingredients:

- 2 racks baby back ribs
- 1 tbsp olive oil
- 1 cup orange juice
- 2 tbsp honey
- 2 tbsp soy sauce
- 1 tsp grated ginger
- 1 tsp garlic powder
- Salt and pepper to taste

Instructions:

1. Preheat grill to medium heat.
2. Rub ribs with olive oil and season with salt and pepper.
3. Grill ribs over indirect heat for 2 hours, turning occasionally.
4. In a saucepan, combine orange juice, honey, soy sauce, ginger, and garlic.
5. Brush ribs with orange glaze during the last 15 minutes of grilling.
6. Serve with extra glaze on the side.

Korean BBQ Ribs

Ingredients:

- 2 racks baby back ribs
- 1 tbsp sesame oil
- 2 tbsp soy sauce
- 2 tbsp brown sugar
- 2 tbsp rice vinegar
- 1 tbsp grated ginger
- 3 cloves garlic, minced
- 1 tsp gochujang (Korean chili paste)
- 1 tbsp sesame seeds
- 1 tbsp green onions, chopped

Instructions:

1. Preheat grill to medium heat.
2. Rub ribs with sesame oil and season with salt and pepper.
3. Grill ribs over indirect heat for 2 hours.
4. In a saucepan, combine soy sauce, brown sugar, rice vinegar, ginger, garlic, and gochujang.
5. Brush ribs with Korean BBQ sauce during the last 15–20 minutes of grilling.
6. Garnish with sesame seeds and green onions before serving.

Pineapple Teriyaki Ribs

Ingredients:

- 2 racks baby back ribs
- 1 tbsp olive oil
- 1 cup teriyaki sauce
- 1 cup pineapple juice
- 2 tbsp brown sugar
- 1 tbsp grated ginger
- 2 tbsp soy sauce
- 1 tsp garlic powder

Instructions:

1. Preheat grill to medium heat.
2. Rub ribs with olive oil and grill for 2 hours, turning occasionally.
3. In a saucepan, combine teriyaki sauce, pineapple juice, brown sugar, ginger, soy sauce, and garlic powder.
4. Brush pineapple teriyaki sauce over ribs during the last 15–20 minutes of grilling.
5. Serve with extra sauce on the side.

Maple Chipotle Grilled Ribs

Ingredients:

- 2 racks baby back ribs
- 1 tbsp olive oil
- 2 tbsp maple syrup
- 1 tbsp chipotle chili powder
- 1 tsp garlic powder
- 1 tsp smoked paprika
- 1 tbsp apple cider vinegar
- Salt and pepper to taste

Instructions:

1. Preheat grill to medium heat.
2. Rub ribs with olive oil and season with salt and pepper.
3. Grill ribs over indirect heat for 2 hours, flipping occasionally.
4. In a bowl, combine maple syrup, chipotle chili powder, garlic powder, paprika, apple cider vinegar, and salt.
5. Brush maple chipotle glaze over ribs during the last 15 minutes of grilling.
6. Serve with extra glaze.

Cajun-Spiced BBQ Ribs

Ingredients:

- 2 racks baby back ribs
- 1 tbsp olive oil
- 2 tbsp Cajun seasoning
- 1 tsp garlic powder
- 1 tsp onion powder
- 1 tsp paprika
- 1 tsp thyme
- 1 tsp brown sugar
- 1 cup BBQ sauce

Instructions:

1. Preheat grill to medium heat.
2. Rub ribs with olive oil and Cajun seasoning, garlic powder, onion powder, paprika, thyme, and brown sugar.
3. Grill ribs over indirect heat for 2 hours, turning occasionally.
4. Brush BBQ sauce over ribs during the last 10 minutes of grilling.
5. Serve with extra sauce on the side.

Grilled BBQ Ribs with Whiskey Sauce

Ingredients:

- 2 racks baby back ribs
- 1 tbsp olive oil
- 1 cup BBQ sauce
- ¼ cup whiskey
- 2 tbsp brown sugar
- 1 tbsp Dijon mustard
- 1 tsp Worcestershire sauce

Instructions:

1. Preheat grill to medium heat.
2. Rub ribs with olive oil and grill over indirect heat for 2 hours.
3. In a saucepan, combine BBQ sauce, whiskey, brown sugar, Dijon mustard, and Worcestershire sauce.
4. Brush whiskey BBQ sauce over ribs during the last 10–15 minutes of grilling.
5. Serve with extra whiskey sauce on the side.

Grilled Ribs with Brown Sugar and Mustard

Ingredients:

- 2 racks baby back ribs
- 1 tbsp olive oil
- ¼ cup brown sugar
- 2 tbsp Dijon mustard
- 2 tbsp apple cider vinegar
- 1 tsp garlic powder
- Salt and pepper to taste

Instructions:

1. Preheat grill to medium heat.
2. Rub ribs with olive oil and season with salt and pepper.
3. Grill ribs over indirect heat for 2 hours, flipping occasionally.
4. In a bowl, mix brown sugar, Dijon mustard, apple cider vinegar, and garlic powder.
5. Brush the brown sugar mustard glaze over ribs during the last 15–20 minutes of grilling.
6. Serve with extra glaze on the side.

Texas-Style BBQ Ribs

Ingredients:

- 2 racks baby back ribs
- 1 tbsp olive oil
- 2 tbsp chili powder
- 1 tbsp paprika
- 1 tsp garlic powder
- 1 tsp onion powder
- 1 tsp cumin
- 1 tsp brown sugar
- 1 cup BBQ sauce

Instructions:

1. Preheat grill to medium heat.
2. Rub ribs with olive oil and season with chili powder, paprika, garlic powder, onion powder, cumin, and brown sugar.
3. Grill ribs over indirect heat for 2 hours, turning occasionally.
4. Brush with BBQ sauce during the last 15 minutes of grilling.
5. Serve with extra BBQ sauce on the side.

Grilled Ribs with Tangy BBQ Sauce

Ingredients:

- 2 racks baby back ribs
- 1 tbsp olive oil
- 1 cup BBQ sauce
- 1 tbsp apple cider vinegar
- 1 tbsp Dijon mustard
- 1 tsp lemon juice

Instructions:

1. Preheat grill to medium heat.
2. Rub ribs with olive oil and grill over indirect heat for 2 hours, turning occasionally.
3. In a bowl, combine BBQ sauce, apple cider vinegar, Dijon mustard, and lemon juice for the tangy sauce.
4. Brush tangy BBQ sauce over ribs during the last 10 minutes of grilling.
5. Serve with extra sauce on the side.

Herb-Crusted BBQ Ribs

Ingredients:

- 2 racks baby back ribs
- 1 tbsp olive oil
- 2 tbsp fresh rosemary, chopped
- 1 tbsp fresh thyme, chopped
- 1 tbsp garlic powder
- 1 tsp salt
- 1 tsp black pepper
- 1 cup BBQ sauce

Instructions:

1. Preheat grill to medium heat.
2. Rub ribs with olive oil and season with rosemary, thyme, garlic powder, salt, and pepper.
3. Grill ribs over indirect heat for 2 hours, flipping occasionally.
4. Brush with BBQ sauce during the last 15 minutes of grilling.
5. Serve with extra sauce and fresh herbs.

Spicy Sriracha BBQ Ribs

Ingredients:

- 2 racks baby back ribs
- 1 tbsp olive oil
- ¼ cup Sriracha sauce
- ¼ cup BBQ sauce
- 2 tbsp honey
- 2 cloves garlic, minced
- 1 tsp ginger, grated
- 1 tbsp soy sauce

Instructions:

1. Preheat grill to medium heat.
2. Rub ribs with olive oil and grill over indirect heat for 2 hours.
3. In a bowl, mix Sriracha sauce, BBQ sauce, honey, garlic, ginger, and soy sauce.
4. Brush the spicy Sriracha BBQ sauce over ribs during the last 15–20 minutes of grilling.
5. Serve with extra sauce on the side.

Smoked Bourbon BBQ Ribs

Ingredients:

- 2 racks baby back ribs
- 1 tbsp olive oil
- ¼ cup bourbon
- 1 cup BBQ sauce
- 2 tbsp brown sugar
- 1 tbsp Dijon mustard
- 1 tsp garlic powder
- 1 tbsp apple cider vinegar

Instructions:

1. Preheat smoker to 225°F.
2. Rub ribs with olive oil and season with salt and pepper.
3. Smoke ribs for 4 hours, turning occasionally.
4. In a saucepan, combine bourbon, BBQ sauce, brown sugar, Dijon mustard, garlic powder, and apple cider vinegar.
5. Brush bourbon BBQ sauce over ribs during the last 15 minutes of smoking.
6. Serve with extra sauce.

Grilled BBQ Ribs with Spicy Rub

Ingredients:

- 2 racks baby back ribs
- 1 tbsp olive oil
- 2 tbsp chili powder
- 1 tsp cayenne pepper
- 1 tsp smoked paprika
- 1 tsp garlic powder
- 1 tbsp brown sugar
- Salt and black pepper to taste

Instructions:

1. Preheat grill to medium heat.
2. Rub ribs with olive oil and coat with spicy rub mixture (chili powder, cayenne, paprika, garlic powder, brown sugar, salt, and pepper).
3. Grill ribs over indirect heat for 2 hours, flipping occasionally.
4. Brush with BBQ sauce during the last 15 minutes of grilling.
5. Serve with extra sauce on the side.

Zesty Lime BBQ Ribs

Ingredients:

- 2 racks baby back ribs
- 1 tbsp olive oil
- 1 tbsp lime zest
- 2 tbsp lime juice
- 2 tbsp brown sugar
- 1 tbsp chili powder
- 1 tsp garlic powder
- 1 tsp cumin

Instructions:

1. Preheat grill to medium heat.
2. Rub ribs with olive oil and season with lime zest, lime juice, brown sugar, chili powder, garlic powder, cumin, salt, and pepper.
3. Grill ribs over indirect heat for 2 hours, turning occasionally.
4. Serve with extra lime wedges on the side.

Grilled Baby Back Ribs with Cilantro Lime Butter

Ingredients:

- 2 racks baby back ribs
- 1 tbsp olive oil
- 1 cup unsalted butter, softened
- 2 tbsp cilantro, chopped
- 1 tbsp lime juice
- 1 tsp lime zest
- 1 tsp garlic powder

Instructions:

1. Preheat grill to medium heat.
2. Rub ribs with olive oil and grill over indirect heat for 2 hours, flipping occasionally.
3. In a bowl, mix softened butter with cilantro, lime juice, lime zest, and garlic powder.
4. Brush cilantro lime butter over ribs during the last 10 minutes of grilling.
5. Serve with extra cilantro lime butter on the side.

Grilled Ribs with Sweet Honey Garlic Sauce

Ingredients:

- 2 racks baby back ribs
- 1 tbsp olive oil
- ½ cup honey
- 3 cloves garlic, minced
- 1 tbsp soy sauce
- 1 tbsp apple cider vinegar
- 1 tsp ginger, grated

Instructions:

1. Preheat grill to medium heat.
2. Rub ribs with olive oil and grill over indirect heat for 2 hours, flipping occasionally.
3. In a saucepan, combine honey, garlic, soy sauce, vinegar, and ginger.
4. Brush honey garlic sauce over ribs during the last 10–15 minutes of grilling.
5. Serve with extra sauce on the side.

Citrus Glazed BBQ Ribs

Ingredients:

- 2 racks baby back ribs
- 1 tbsp olive oil
- 1 cup orange juice
- ¼ cup lemon juice
- 2 tbsp honey
- 1 tbsp Dijon mustard
- 1 tsp garlic powder
- 1 tsp rosemary, chopped

Instructions:

1. Preheat grill to medium heat.
2. Rub ribs with olive oil and grill over indirect heat for 2 hours, turning occasionally.
3. In a saucepan, combine orange juice, lemon juice, honey, Dijon mustard, garlic powder, and rosemary.
4. Brush citrus glaze over ribs during the last 10 minutes of grilling.
5. Serve with extra glaze on the side.

Grilled Ribs with Spicy Peach Sauce

Ingredients:

- 2 racks baby back ribs
- 1 tbsp olive oil
- 1 cup peach preserves
- 2 tbsp apple cider vinegar
- 1 tsp cayenne pepper
- 1 tbsp Worcestershire sauce
- Salt and pepper to taste

Instructions:

1. Preheat grill to medium heat.
2. Rub ribs with olive oil and grill over indirect heat for 2 hours, flipping occasionally.
3. In a saucepan, combine peach preserves, apple cider vinegar, cayenne, Worcestershire sauce, salt, and pepper.
4. Brush spicy peach sauce over ribs during the last 15 minutes of grilling.
5. Serve with extra sauce on the side.

Garlic and Rosemary BBQ Ribs

Ingredients:

- 2 racks baby back ribs
- 1 tbsp olive oil
- 3 cloves garlic, minced
- 2 tbsp fresh rosemary, chopped
- 1 tbsp lemon juice
- 1 tsp garlic powder
- Salt and black pepper to taste

Instructions:

1. Preheat grill to medium heat.
2. Rub ribs with olive oil and season with garlic, rosemary, garlic powder, salt, and pepper.
3. Grill ribs over indirect heat for 2 hours, flipping occasionally.
4. Brush with BBQ sauce during the last 15 minutes of grilling.
5. Serve with extra rosemary and garlic.

Cajun Honey BBQ Ribs

Ingredients:

- 2 racks baby back ribs
- 1 tbsp olive oil
- 2 tbsp Cajun seasoning
- 2 tbsp honey
- 1 tbsp apple cider vinegar
- 1 tbsp Dijon mustard
- 1 tsp smoked paprika

Instructions:

1. Preheat grill to medium heat.
2. Rub ribs with olive oil and Cajun seasoning.
3. Grill ribs over indirect heat for 2 hours, turning occasionally.
4. In a bowl, mix honey, apple cider vinegar, Dijon mustard, and smoked paprika.
5. Brush Cajun honey BBQ sauce over ribs during the last 15–20 minutes of grilling.
6. Serve with extra sauce on the side.

Sweet BBQ Grilled Ribs with Pecan Glaze

Ingredients:

- 2 racks baby back ribs
- 1 tbsp olive oil
- ¼ cup brown sugar
- ½ cup BBQ sauce
- ¼ cup pecan halves, finely chopped
- 1 tbsp honey
- 1 tsp vanilla extract
- 1 tbsp Dijon mustard

Instructions:

1. Preheat grill to medium heat.
2. Rub ribs with olive oil and grill over indirect heat for 2 hours, turning occasionally.
3. In a saucepan, combine brown sugar, BBQ sauce, honey, vanilla, Dijon mustard, and chopped pecans.
4. Brush pecan glaze over ribs during the last 15 minutes of grilling.
5. Serve with extra pecan glaze on the side.

Smoked Maple BBQ Ribs

Ingredients:

- 2 racks baby back ribs
- 1 tbsp olive oil
- 1 cup maple syrup
- ¼ cup apple cider vinegar
- 2 tbsp Dijon mustard
- 1 tbsp Worcestershire sauce
- 1 tsp smoked paprika
- 1 tsp garlic powder

Instructions:

1. Preheat smoker to 225°F.
2. Rub ribs with olive oil and season with salt and pepper.
3. Smoke ribs for 4 hours, turning occasionally.
4. In a saucepan, combine maple syrup, apple cider vinegar, Dijon mustard, Worcestershire sauce, smoked paprika, and garlic powder.
5. Brush maple BBQ sauce over ribs during the last 15 minutes of smoking.
6. Serve with extra maple sauce on the side.

Grilled BBQ Ribs with Sweet and Sour Sauce

Ingredients:

- 2 racks baby back ribs
- 1 tbsp olive oil
- ½ cup BBQ sauce
- ¼ cup pineapple juice
- 2 tbsp honey
- 2 tbsp rice vinegar
- 1 tbsp soy sauce
- 1 tsp ginger, grated

Instructions:

1. Preheat grill to medium heat.
2. Rub ribs with olive oil and grill over indirect heat for 2 hours, flipping occasionally.
3. In a saucepan, combine BBQ sauce, pineapple juice, honey, rice vinegar, soy sauce, and ginger.
4. Brush sweet and sour sauce over ribs during the last 15 minutes of grilling.
5. Serve with extra sauce on the side.

Grilled Ribs with Chimichurri Sauce

Ingredients:

- 2 racks baby back ribs
- 1 tbsp olive oil
- 1 cup fresh parsley, chopped
- 2 tbsp red wine vinegar
- 4 cloves garlic, minced
- 1 tsp red pepper flakes
- 1 tsp oregano
- ½ cup olive oil

Instructions:

1. Preheat grill to medium heat.
2. Rub ribs with olive oil and grill over indirect heat for 2 hours, turning occasionally.
3. In a bowl, mix parsley, red wine vinegar, garlic, red pepper flakes, oregano, and olive oil to make chimichurri sauce.
4. Brush chimichurri sauce over ribs during the last 10–15 minutes of grilling.
5. Serve with extra chimichurri on the side.

Slow Cooked BBQ Ribs

Ingredients:

- 2 racks baby back ribs
- 1 tbsp olive oil
- 1 cup BBQ sauce
- 2 tbsp brown sugar
- 1 tbsp apple cider vinegar
- 1 tbsp mustard

Instructions:

1. Preheat oven to 300°F.
2. Rub ribs with olive oil and season with salt and pepper.
3. Wrap ribs in foil and bake for 2.5–3 hours.
4. In a saucepan, combine BBQ sauce, brown sugar, apple cider vinegar, and mustard.
5. Brush ribs with sauce and bake for an additional 15–20 minutes.
6. Serve with extra sauce.

Grilled Ribs with Smoky Tomato Sauce

Ingredients:

- 2 racks baby back ribs
- 1 tbsp olive oil
- 1 cup tomato sauce
- 2 tbsp apple cider vinegar
- 1 tbsp smoked paprika
- 1 tsp garlic powder
- 1 tbsp Worcestershire sauce

Instructions:

1. Preheat grill to medium heat.
2. Rub ribs with olive oil and grill over indirect heat for 2 hours.
3. In a saucepan, combine tomato sauce, apple cider vinegar, smoked paprika, garlic powder, and Worcestershire sauce.
4. Brush smoky tomato sauce over ribs during the last 10–15 minutes of grilling.
5. Serve with extra sauce.

Grilled BBQ Ribs with Raspberry Chipotle Sauce

Ingredients:

- 2 racks baby back ribs
- 1 tbsp olive oil
- ½ cup raspberry preserves
- 2 tbsp chipotle in adobo, chopped
- 2 tbsp apple cider vinegar
- 1 tbsp honey

Instructions:

1. Preheat grill to medium heat.
2. Rub ribs with olive oil and grill over indirect heat for 2 hours, flipping occasionally.
3. In a saucepan, combine raspberry preserves, chipotle in adobo, apple cider vinegar, and honey.
4. Brush raspberry chipotle sauce over ribs during the last 15 minutes of grilling.
5. Serve with extra sauce on the side.

Smoky Pineapple BBQ Ribs

Ingredients:

- 2 racks baby back ribs
- 1 tbsp olive oil
- 1 cup pineapple juice
- ¼ cup brown sugar
- 1 tbsp soy sauce
- 1 tsp smoked paprika
- 1 tsp garlic powder

Instructions:

1. Preheat grill to medium heat.
2. Rub ribs with olive oil and grill over indirect heat for 2 hours, turning occasionally.
3. In a saucepan, combine pineapple juice, brown sugar, soy sauce, smoked paprika, and garlic powder.
4. Brush smoky pineapple BBQ sauce over ribs during the last 15 minutes of grilling.
5. Serve with extra sauce on the side.

Thai BBQ Grilled Ribs

Ingredients:

- 2 racks baby back ribs
- 1 tbsp olive oil
- ¼ cup fish sauce
- 2 tbsp lime juice
- 1 tbsp brown sugar
- 2 cloves garlic, minced
- 1 tsp grated ginger
- 1 tbsp soy sauce

Instructions:

1. Preheat grill to medium heat.
2. Rub ribs with olive oil and grill over indirect heat for 2 hours.
3. In a bowl, combine fish sauce, lime juice, brown sugar, garlic, ginger, and soy sauce.
4. Brush Thai BBQ sauce over ribs during the last 10–15 minutes of grilling.
5. Serve with extra sauce and lime wedges.

Grilled BBQ Ribs with Roasted Garlic Sauce

Ingredients:

- 2 racks baby back ribs
- 1 tbsp olive oil
- 1 bulb garlic, roasted and mashed
- ¼ cup BBQ sauce
- 1 tbsp olive oil
- 1 tbsp balsamic vinegar
- Salt and pepper to taste

Instructions:

1. Preheat grill to medium heat.
2. Rub ribs with olive oil and grill over indirect heat for 2 hours, turning occasionally.
3. In a bowl, mix mashed roasted garlic, BBQ sauce, olive oil, balsamic vinegar, salt, and pepper.
4. Brush roasted garlic sauce over ribs during the last 10–15 minutes of grilling.
5. Serve with extra roasted garlic sauce on the side.